Series Editor - Sylvia P. Webb

Sylvia Webb is a well known consultant, author and lecturer in the information management field. Her first book 'Creating an Information Service' in its third edition, was published by Aslib and has sold in over forty countries. She has experience of working in both the public and private sectors, ranging from public libraries to national and international organisations. She has also been a lecturer at Ashridge Management College, specialising in management and inter-personal skills, which led to her second book, 'Personal Development in Information Work', also published by Aslib. She has served on a number of government advisory bodies and is past Chair of the Information and Library Services Lead Body which develops National Vocational Qualifications (NVQs) for the LIS profession. She is actively involved in professional education with Aslib and the Library Association and is also a former Vice-President of the Institute of Information Scientists. As well as being editor of this series, Sylvia Webb has also written two of the Know How Guides: '*Making a charge for library and information services*' and '*Preparing a guide to your library and information service*'.

A list of titles in the Aslib Know How Series
appears on the back cover of this volume.

Acknowledgments

This is my opportunity to say "thank you" for the knowledge and help both of us have had from, and the informed discussion we've enjoyed with many people (especially those on Aslib's "Marketing the information service" course, which we direct) while revising this guide. Although I am a "lapsed" librarian, the one thing I have never forgotten is how supportive and encouraging my professional colleauges have always been. However, we would particularly like to thank Helen Clemow, Nick Parsons, Paul Pedley and Caroline Plaice for "volunteering" to provide case studies. Also our publisher, Sarah Blair, whose infinite understanding of the idiosyncrasies of a consultant's life (which usually result in missed deadlines) must be second to none in the publishing world.

Closer to home, thanks go to Robin Gray for proof-reading and ruthless but constructive comments; also Bridget's husband Andrew Batchelor and my mother Eileen for providing objective input and TLC, particularly the reviving but non-alcoholic late-evening brew of which I have become inordinately fond.

Contents

1. Introduction to the Second edition

Since Helen wrote the first edition in the Autumn of 1993, many things have changed for information managers, not least what they prefer to be called. Four years ago, the word "librarian" and "library" were accepted common parlance. Now, most information professionals we meet refer to "information managers" and their "LIS" (or some variation on those initials). In response, we have used these phrases throughout the book - a reversal of Helen's approach last time.

The main change, of course, has been in the technology of delivery systems. We have moved on through on-line to CD-ROMs and the Internet has almost come out of nowhere. But does any of this fundamentally affect the effective marketing of the information service? Our answer is "No". Marketing always will be about understanding and effectively meeting the needs of customers in a competitive environment. The means by which you deliver your services may change over time, new services may be devised and old ones dropped. But the essential marketing disciplines of planning to meet your preferred customers' needs and then going out to bring those customers in through your door through good promotion and excellent service remain.

This book is about those disciplines. We make no apology for covering the basics for those who are new to marketing. But we have added sections on customer focus, business development and relationship marketing, to reflect the developments which have gone on in the broader business community. And we have, of course, added a section on the Internet to the promotion section.

Marketing is fun. Marketing is about thriving in difficult times. But above all, marketing is about doing things. You can read all the books in the world, but if you don't put the advice into practice, nothing will happen. There are customers out there who need you - we hope that you will find them more easily and serve them better as a result of reading this book.

Bridget Batchelor and Helen Coote, October 1997

2. What is marketing?

There are many definitions of the term marketing, some slick ("marketing is 90% common sense"), some profound ("marketing is a state of mind which informs corporate priorities"), some based on jargon ("establishing a competitive edge"). However, the Chartered Institute of Marketing's definition "the management process responsible for the identifying, anticipating and satisfying customer requirements profitably" covers the key elements of focusing on the customer's existing and future needs, in a way which is of benefit to the service provider.

There are a number of key activities which must be undertaken:

- researching and analysing the existing marketplace in which the LIS can offer its services
- identifying what the needs are and which parts of that marketplace share them
- analysing the LIS's strengths and weaknesses in terms of resources, personnel and areas of specialist expertise
- understanding the competition
- designing offerings (i.e. services and products) which translate the LIS's internal strengths into specific services that meet the identified customer needs
- making existing and potential customers aware of these offerings
- monitoring and/or measuring customer satisfaction with the services provided, feeding back and acting on the resultant information.

These activities cannot be undertaken as a one-off exercise. The market-place, the customers' needs and perceptions, the activities of the competition and the LIS's own attributes and resources change over time and in response to one another. The whole marketing effort is continuous, although there are peaks and troughs in any one of the component activities. It is a dynamic process.

For example, collecting and analysing data about clients and competitors in order to prepare your first marketing strategy is a major exercise. But once done, it only has to be up-dated; and you only write a strategy every 2-3 years. Drawing up your marketing action plan is part of the annual planning cycle, although its effectiveness must be routinely monitored. Media relations require constant attention, as does the day-to-day "selling" of your service. But you only need a new brochure every 18 months or so.

All of these activities are marketing. It is a mixture of planning and analysis, and on-going action. It is also a management process, not a separate function undertaken (possibly part-time) by the "marketing person". It should be an LIS-wide philosophy, accepted by everyone from top management down, because only in that way can the two tests of any proposed action ("does it benefit the customers?" and "does it benefit us?") carry any weight.

Contemporary marketing is customer-focussed, which means that you base the design and delivery of your services as far as possible on what the customers want, not what you happen to have available. It reflects the change in approach to customer service which has taken place during the 1990s. Customers are now becoming accustomed to good customer service in many aspects of their lives. At first it was introduced by companies aiming to achieve competitive advantage. Now it is a requirement which no-one in business can afford to ignore. At one time, the aim was to have "happy" customers. Then we were expected to have "satisfied" customers, but now we are exhorted to "delight" them.

"Delighting" customers involves a lot more than just meeting their information needs. Crucially, it includes delivering the service in the way which is most suited to their needs, and ensuring that all aspects of their experience of dealing with the LIS are at or above a standard which they have helped to set. This involves ruthless use of the fundamental marketing technique of segmentation, which we describe in the next chapter. Segmentation enables you to understand the needs of groups (or segments) of customers in the required depth. Without it, you are likely to treat all customers the same which is a sure way of not satisfying - let alone delighting - a number of them.

A customer-facing approach to marketing can only be effective if the LIS's values (or mission) statement and overall objectives are expressed in compatible terms. For example, if objectives are primarily of the "Acquisitions will be catalogued within no more than 10 days of receipt" variety, then staff effort will (not unnaturally) be focussed on achieving them, rather than working on ways of, for example, "Achieving customer satisfaction ratings for stock currency of 94%".

Objectives come in many forms. They can be set for you, or you can determine them yourself. But, since the aim of the marketing strategy is to achieve them, they must be carefully prioritised. The resources (both people and financial) available, the time span and the pressures from senior management, may mean that only three or four objectives will be top priority. The important factor is that each objective is, and is seen to be, achievable. There is nothing more demoralising than projects that go off at half speed, fail completely or have poor quality results because the resources were spread too thinly. Today, many information managers have the added incentive of personal performance points; ill-defined or over-optimistic objectives will not lead to winning many of them. But above all objectives should be SMART - Simple, Measurable, Achievable, Realistic and able to be Timetabled.

The values statement describes what the organisation stands for and is a long-term statement of purposes. A broader concept than the mission statement which it replaces, it addresses the following questions:

- what is our business?
- how do we do business?
- what are we trying to achieve?
- how do we relate to our stakeholders - the people who have an interest in or influence over the success of the LIS?

An LIS can have a values statement of its own, but it must complement that of its parent organisation. Ideally, all the staff should be involved in its preparation so that it reflects what *they* feel about *their* LIS and where is it going. However it must also faithfully reflect what you are offering. If, for example, your values statement implies a significant IT capacity, then the library has to have the technology and the supporting software/database capability and expertise to answer the queries that will come its way. And if it is overtly customer-focussed, then steps must be taken before it is made publicly available to ensure that all staff know:

- what the supporting standards of service are
- what behaviours are required of them to meet those standards
- how performance is to be monitored
- what training they are going to receive to enable them to meet the standards.

Many customer care programmes have foundered because organisations launched the initiative without first informing and training the staff. Customers' expectations were raised, only to be dashed when they noticed no obvious changes in the way they were dealt with.

This book assumes a customer-facing approach to marketing, because that is contemporary best practice. But it is better to go for the older-style of marketing, and get that right, than to try and change too much, too quickly and not succeed. Customer-facing marketing pays dividends in increased customer loyalty, but it is riskier if you get it wrong.

3. Marketing strategy

Marketing is a business process and has the same six basic steps as any other process i.e. to:

- set objectives
- devise an overall strategy
- prepare supporting action plans
- implement the plans
- monitor success and feedback the results
- modify the plans.

Since this book is about marketing, we will focus on the second and third steps. The other steps are down to you - all we will say is that if you don't take those steps, then you might as well not bother with the first three.

First, a resume of what makes any good commercial-style strategy or plan:

- *short*-so that it will be read. long plans are not appreciated, particularly by those who have to implement them
- *adequately researched*- so that there are no inaccuracies or hostages to fortune for potential opponents to latch on to
- *contains achievable milestones and targets*- so that progress in implementing it can be measured
- *written*- so that everyone involved can know what is expected of them, and gain management commitment
- *useable and used*- it should be well-thumbed and dog-eared, because it is the guide to what the LIS staff are doing and is also used as a management tool to monitor progress and adjust action in the light of results.

The key elements of a marketing strategy are as follows:

- assessment of who the customers are, the services they want, their expectations of an LIS, and the benefits they are seeking

- analysis of the LIS's strengths, weaknesses and opportunities and the services it provides

- assessment of the strengths and weaknesses of the competition

- understanding what the real differences are between the LIS and the competition

- a practical action plan which draws on this understanding of the marketplace and sets out measurable actions to achieve the current objectives.

The first three of these enable you to understand and control the triangular relationship between you, your customers and the competition which is fundamental to any business. The lines and angles in the triangle will vary over time for different groups of customers - but if you know what they are and what you are aiming for them to be, then you can plan what needs to be done.

As an example, a library has acquired a new on-line database. The triangle for that product and the existing customers, some of whom have access to their own on-line facilities would be this shape:

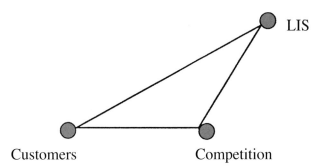

After promoting the new service, the triangle would look more like this:

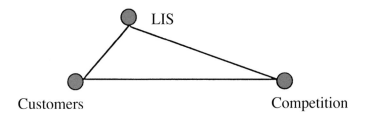

Customers

A customer-facing marketing strategy is based on a deep knowledge of the target customer base. This is, to some extent a chicken and egg situation, since you need to have a certain amount of information before you can decide who your target customers are. But your values statement and/or corporate strategy should define the broad scope of your customers with such phrases as "We will serve the business information needs of the residents of Barsetshire" or "From the London IRC we will serve the needs of UK-based staff". In these circumstances, your marketing strategy need not take account of the residents of neighbouring counties, or staff based in other countries.

However, within those broad definitions, there will be some customers whom you will find more valuable than others, and/or whom you can serve more effectively. In order to decide who they are, and how you can serve both those categories and others, you need certain key information:

- who are they?
- what are their characteristics?
- what triggers their decision to use the LIS?
- what services do they want now?
- what services will they want in the future?
- what services might they be persuaded to buy in the future?
- what are their perceptions and expectations?
- what benefits are they looking for?
- what are their buying factors?

In commercial terms, this will enable you to decide how big the market-place is, how much of it you want to capture ("market share") and what services you are going to offer in order to achieve that.

Who are our customers? The first two types of information enable you to segment your market-place, or divide it into groups with certain characteristics in common. The groups should be large enough to be meaningful and small enough to be manageable in terms of developing marketing plans to serve them. Do not go overboard with too much detail - one of the traps in marketing is to wallow in this stage. If you divide up your marketplace into too many segments, you will not be able to devise a workable plan to serve them all effectively.

You can choose whatever combination of characteristics you like - there are no absolute rules. Some common types are:

- age
- economic group
- SIC code
- geographical location
- company size
- company structure (single site, multi-national etc.)
- how often do customers need to buy

The LIS segmentation might also include:

- speed and frequency of required response
- information handling skills
- attitude to external information providers
- role and position in the customer organisation.

The basis of segmentation will change depending on the purpose of the exercise. If you are trying to decide whether to introduce a computer-based service, you will need to know how many of your potential customers are computer-literate, because that will determine the resources needed for training and will also shape the promotional campaign. But computer-literacy may be irrelevant when assessing the format of a revamped Current Awareness Bulletin unless it is to be delivered electronically.

Correct segmentation is the basis of your entire marketing strategy. All of the rest of the strategic thinking is done in relation to the segments you select, because the needs, wants, expectations and perceptions of each segment will differ from one another, as will the benefits that they are looking for and their Critical Success Factors. The information about all these aspects will affect your assessment of the attractiveness of those markets over time and your ability to compete in them.

The definition of a customer operates at two levels. Customers are organisations - local companies, the finance department, the engineering faculty - but they are also the people who make up those organisations. It is vital, for example, for business librarians to understand not just which companies might use their services, so that they can, say, plan the right core stock but also who the people are within those companies who actually need the information, and who is responsible for getting it.

They may well be different, their attitudes quite diverse, and you will therefore need different approaches to promote (and sell) your service effectively. For example, the sales manager's main concern may be the availability of on-line data about key target customers, while the researcher may need a long back run of statistics. It is no good concentrating your selling efforts on the junior managers who deals with you on a day-to-day basis if they have no control over the budget and never takes decisions. You will also need to cultivate their bosses - the real decision takes.

Customer needs   In looking at the services customers need, you will need to understand not only what they say they want (the "presenting need"), but also what drives that - the issues facing *them* in the environment in which *they* are operating. What are the main issues in their industries? Where are they on their industry's economic cycle? How important is import penetration? Where are the most likely export markets? Have they been affected by new regulations? This understanding - perhaps developed by different members of staff for different industries, or different departments in your company - will enable you not only to provide a higher quality (i.e. more informed) service, but also take a view on their future needs, and plan to meet them.

The smart information manager will look at the likely changes in demand over the strategy period (usually 3 years) and will not only have identified and laid on the right sources but ensured that the customers know that the service is available. A useful tool in understanding market changes is the PEST analysis - an assessment of the Political, Economic, Sociological and Technological changes which are likely to affect the market-place over the strategy period. Political does not have to mean party political. Within a company it could include organisational developments. Similarly Sociological changes do not always mean crime statistics or trends in the number of people over 55. They can include cultural change or shifts in the numbers of staff at a particular site.

Expectations and perceptions A customer's decision to use an LIS - and yours in particular - will depend on their expectation of whether it will help them do whatever they have to do, and their perception of your service. Their expectation will have been formed by a variety of factors, not all of them under your control. These naturally include their own experiences of any type of library and what they have heard from others about LIS in general and yours in particular. But they also include their experiences with other types of service, not necessarily in the information field. For example, someone who has no time for in-house service providers because the IT department has not managed to fix the computer could have a low expectation of the LIS.

Their perceptions of your service is however much more under your control, because it is based on what you actually do and say. It is therefore essential that the quality of service that customers experience is both consistent and matches what your promotional messages say. It is also important to remember that perception and reality may not be the same thing. "One man's steak is another man's BSE infection" represents two perfectly legitimate views of the same meal - the marketing person bears in mind that the two perceptions are both true to those who hold them, and acts accordingly.

Benefits A key marketing concept is that "customers buy the benefits". Put simply, this means that people do not buy the features of a product or service (a flat surface supported by legs is a table) they buy *what it can do for them* - somewhere to eat/work/play card games at a convenient height. So a large family of tall people will be looking for a big table with long legs. Benefits can be practical, as in the example of the table, or more emotional/qualitative. When someone buys a Porsche, they do not buy necessarily a means of private transport -a Mini would provide that. They buy a status symbol - it makes them feel good.

The purpose of understanding the benefits is to enable suppliers to describe their offerings more effectively, because they are addressing the real reasons behind customers' buying choices.

What benefits are LIS customers likely to be looking for? It depends on who they are and their circumstances, but some examples might be:

Customer	Benefit	Feature of service
Sales person	Win crucial order	Quick answers
Student	Pass exams	Enough key sources
Managing Director	Successful expansion	Added value to basic statistics
Council Leader	Enhanced image	Up-to-date information for speech.

Customer buying factors Different groups of customers will choose a specific information source for a particular purpose for different reasons. These buying factors (sometimes called Critical Success Factors) may well be linked to the benefits, and can include ease of access, reliability, price, speed of delivery. By understanding them, and making sure your service meets as many as possible, you increase the likelihood of customers choosing you as their information provider.

Customers choose a particular supplier for different reasons at different times. A business executive wanting information about a potential new market will have priority requirements for the speed of delivery and accuracy of the information. On the other hand a student doing a project is more concerned about the quality and availability of the book stock and help with finding sources of information. But all customers buy from a supplier who is different from and better than all the available courses of action at any particular time. When you last bought a shirt, you liked the colour best, or it was a bargain offer, or you were short of time and had to get it in the nearest shop. It was different in some way from all the other shirts in the world at that particular time.

Successful suppliers are those who persuade customers that they are different and better more often - they "differentiate" themselves more clearly. This is the third key marketing concept (following segmentation and selling the benefits not the features of the service). So, in addition to your knowledge of your strengths and weaknesses (which you keep to yourself), you must also decide what makes your service different *in a way which interests the customers.* Is it that the enquiry desk is continuously staffed from 8.30am to 6.30pm? Are your on-line facilities more user-friendly? Or is it that you have a better range of European daily papers?

This concept of differentiation plays an important part in positioning the LIS. It also explains why it is important to identify your Unique Selling Points (USPs) - the aspects of your service which are unique to you in ways which are important to customers. If you can prove to a group of customers that you understand and can work with their highly complex technical jargon, they are more likely to come to you rather than someone who does not have that ability. However, that skill is irrelevant to another group whose need is for a rapid current awareness service. USPs form the basis of all communication with the customers to whom they are relevant, and clear identification, and protection, of them is a strategic issue.

Competition

The competitors for the LIS may be less obvious than, for example, for a shop or widget manufacturer. But nevertheless, it is important to understand who they are and what their strengths and weaknesses are, so that you can counter them with your own offerings and promotional activities.

Examples of where direct competition can come from includes customers who have their own on-line databases/CD-ROM facilities, Businesslink, and information brokers. It is not unknown for different parts of the same company to be using different sources for essentially similar data. Less obvious competitors are individual customers' own information sources, such as personal subscriptions to journals and networks of contacts.

Research into where your customers obtain the sort of information they clearly need and you provide currently, how they use it and how satisfied they are with the result will enable you to focus and promote your own service more effectively. You can - and must - build up a picture of how well the alternative information sources meet the customer buying factors (CBFs), as well as knowing what service they are offering and its characteristics. Is the competition trying to muscle in on your market-place? Or are your competitors complacent, therefore letting you in to offer a better service to their customers?

A way of representing the strength of the competition in your market-place - actual or potential - is to draw a matrix which lists the CBFs, then rate your own abilities to meet them and those of the competition. Your identified USPs should score highly - if they don't, you need to reconsider them! You should take action on those CBFs where your service does not rate highly against the competition, otherwise any marketing activity to promote that service may be fruitless.

The LIS

The third point of the strategic marketing triangle is the LIS itself - what it is and what it can offer. Undertaking a SWOT (Strengths, Weaknesses, Opportunities and Threats) analysis will focus your mind on what you and your colleagues consider to be the key issues.

Basically, a SWOT is a method of listing the library's key internal strengths and weaknesses, and then relating them to external opportunities and threats. Your SWOT should provide the framework to enable you to organise your thinking, but don't be too subjective or overly optimistic. Otherwise the results will be bland and unfocused - and of absolutely no value whatsoever (marketing or otherwise). Incorporate your knowledge of the customers and the competitors in the opportunities and threats sections.

The SWOT will help you understand what type of organisation you currently are, and what you have the potential to be. The strategic decision is then what you are going to be - what is your position in the market-place to be?

Everyone in business has a position in their market-place, either through choice or by default. Your default position is brought about by the actions of others, who ensure that customers see them in a particular way in relation to other suppliers, including you. A marketing strategy therefore needs to address how you are currently seen, what you want your position to be, and what action is needed to bring about the necessary re-positioning.

You need to concentrate on the areas of the LIS's strengths that can be maximised, and which can be used to improve and hold its position. These may include:

- a reputation for expertise and reliability
- value added services, e.g. a one-off request for information triggers an apt and unsolicited update
- individual service, e.g. information provided is tailored to individual customer's needs
- a better product, e.g. standard printed material is enhanced by the latest on-line services
- a complete product, where *all* the customer's information needs are met from a sophisticated research ability to the provision of a timetable
- the staff, who are perceived as knowledgeable, good communicators with a pleasant approach *and* an understanding of the customer's requirements.

Positioning, like segmentation, is a fundamental marketing technique. It means choosing the type of library service you wish to offer, not functionally (i.e. business, specialist) but in qualitative terms. From this strategic decision flows everything in your marketing plan, because everything you do, say, or write about your library and its services must support and reinforce it. You cannot provide an average service and charge premium service rates. You cannot claim to provide a highly professional, quality service to business and promote it through a brochure stapled together with a crude photocopied cover.

Corporate identity is the most visible element of a marketing strategy. It is more than the decision about a logo or which colour an organisation chooses for its headed paper - it is the visual expression of the positioning and gives subliminal messages to reinforce what is said. Re-positioning is therefore often accompanied by a new corporate identity, which not only makes clear what the new positioning is, but also that there has been a change.

Should the LIS have its own corporate identity? For one which is taking marketing seriously, the answer has to be "Yes", in order to reinforce positioning statements and differentiate it from the competition.

Within the parent organisation house-style, the information manager may be able to negotiate a subsidiary or adapted logo or use of complementary colours. Your ideas should remain faithful to the overall concept of the corporate identity, so that your brochure (or whatever) is clearly seen as a member of the same corporate "family". The LIS offering a totally in-house service may have much more freedom to develop its own house-style. Remember however that you will want to be seen as being "part of the team", and therefore there is a lot of merit in making strong visual references in the corporate identity of the parent organisation.

Summary

The marketing strategy analyses the market-place in which your LIS is operating (customer needs, wants, expectations and perceptions - current and foreseen; the relative strength of the competition) and sets that against its ability to deliver a specified amount of the required services. It then makes decisions about strategic issues, which will include:

- which market segments are we going to serve (including these we are going to leave alone)?
- what are we going to offer them?
- in what volume?
- in what way (service delivery)?
- how are we going to be seen (positioning)?

Some of these decisions will be difficult to take, especially if you have always tried to provide a full service to all-comers. But in times of tightening budgets, there are very few LIS who can continue to do that. A marketing strategy which is based on a scrupulous analysis of the market-place and the LIS' ability (including resources) to serve that market, can be used in management discussions about how the LIS is supported and to what extent. It can be a very powerful tool in your fight to survive in an increasingly competitive world.

4. Marketing planning

The marketing strategy should be as short as is reasonable to do the analysis and state the strategic decisions. It is the context for the supporting action plan, which sets out what you are actually going to do to implement those decisions.

The "4Ps"

The traditional marketing action plan has four elements, known as the "4Ps". They are

product   the right service that performs its intended function well to meet the customers' needs

price   the right price, reflecting the quality of the service(s) offered and the current market conditions

place   how the service is made available to customers

promotion   communication/presentation that appeals to the customer and conveys the right image.

They are the four areas of marketing activity which are considered to be within the marketeer's control, and which can therefore be planned. There are other "Ps" which are important - positioning, politics, public opinion, profit - but they are not suitable as headings in an action plan. Recently, advanced marketing thinking has recognised the importance of people, in these days when customer service is playing an increasingly important role in both selling and retaining customer loyalty. For service providers, the inclusion of this 5th "P" is now a virtual necessity.

This approach comes from the fast-moving consumer goods sector (baked beans, chocolate bars, cars); but selling a service is different in four crucial respects to selling chocolate bars. Before examining the make-up of a marketing plan for a service, therefore, it might help to understand these differences, which are:

- intangibility
- inseparability

- consistency
- perishability.

Intangibility Every service, whether it is offered by an information manager, an accountant or a marketing consultant is distinguished, to a greater or lesser degree, by intangibility. The majority of products can be customer-tested before they are bought, but a customer cannot usually have a trial run before using a service.

However, the information manager is perhaps more fortunate than other professionals. He or she has some tangible offerings, in the form of documents already in stock, computer searches already completed etc. They can be used to enable potential customers assess whether this particular LIS has got what they are looking for, and can be useful to them.

Inseparability Frequently the user of the service does not distinguish between the service itself and the person who is actually providing it, especially when the service is used at the same time as it is offered, i.e. answering an enquiry over the telephone. And the customer is often involved in the service, e.g. by providing enough information to enable a helpful answer to be made to an enquiry. The quality of the service, and customers' decisions about whether to come back, may often depend on their reaction to the individual with whom they dealt, not on the quality of the actual information provided.

Consistency This is allied to inseparability. Because the providers of the service are individuals, they will have differing levels of expertise, methods of communication, subject knowledge and personality. Although certain tasks performed and services offered by a library can be routine, it is not possible to standardise everything. This means that customers are not always able to make comparable judgement of the quality of a service before they decide which one to use, and they have to take a risk. Some people do not find this easy to do, and you must find ways of making it more acceptable.

Perishability Most services have a short shelf life, and cannot be conveniently stored away for future use, because they are offered and used at the same time. This means, for example, that a subject specialist cannot perform an on-line search during a quiet time and then file it away to await an enquiry by which time the information will need updating anyway. Supply and demand come in peaks and troughs, and although some information managers can anticipate this and work around it, for the majority it is a case of balancing resources to meet demand.

These four factors need to be taken into account in developing the marketing plan for an information service. In assessing the portfolio of services, careful thought needs to be given to how they can be made tangible and attractive to customers. Planning for the development of the people will take into account the need for consistency and for staff to reflect this in their client dealings.

There is no mandatory format for a marketing plan. Some successful ones have been written on the back of the proverbial envelope! But however it is written, it should clearly specify who is to do what by when, what resources (of all types) will be available to them and how progress is to be monitored. You should also state the assumptions on which you are writing this plan at this time, so that, if circumstances change, you have a justifiable reason for going back to the drawing board. We have found that the "5 Ps" format works well, and discuss it below.

Portfolio of services Certain services are mandatory, depending on which type of information service you run. You cannot claim to be, for example, a business information service if you do not offer to find basic data about companies. These "core" services are what you are in business to provide, and form the heart of your service portfolio - assuming that there is continued customer demand. It may be that your customers want you to provide more, or less, of certain services. In this part of the plan, you identify the action required to meet not just the type of demand, but also the balance of different types of service.

In addition, you will have a range of "peripheral" services - extras which help to make your service more attractive to customers. The key issue around these is balancing the resources required against their attractiveness to customers, and how they fit with the strategic direction of the LIS. For example, a corporate LIS which wants to re-position itself closer to the decision-making process might re-consider its role as a copying unit or filing section. The services must be of at least a specified minimum standard, which you may be required (or choose) to raise over time. But if you are a centre of excellence, or aiming to be the main supplier of information services in a particular geographical area, then that minimum standard must be well exceeded.

You specify how you are going to develop your portfolio of services in the "product" part of your plan. This may include, of course, dropping one part of the service which is no longer in demand, which you cannot provide within the available resources or which would cost too much to maintain in a competitive market. Being prepared to drop "redundant" services is as important as moving into new areas to meet market demands.

But, building on your knowledge of customer needs, the competition and your LIS's strengths (a particularly good stock of books or databases on specific subjects; a person with acknowledged expertise) you can create, or increase, the difference between your service and that of your competitors. This part of the annual plan enables you to review how well each service matches with customer needs and expectations, and plan the action required to correct any discrepancies.

How does the LIS fit in with all the other services that your customer uses? What triggers their decision to use it? What *exactly* are you offering? and most importantly, does it fit with what they want? It could very well be that your customers are using the service in a way or for a reason that you had not actually intended it to be used. Perhaps, for example, the specialist journals (bought at great expense as learned tomes) are only used on a certain day - when the executive jobs supplements appear!

Price is one of the most difficult issues for information managers. There is still a widespread expectation that information services will be free. If you do not run a free service, the pricing part of your plan should therefore have a number of actions designed to manage that expectation, change it over time and enable the library staff to deal with the issue in the meantime.

As a general rule, customers value what they pay for, and pay for what they value. One approach to charging for information services therefore is to establish your service as being of significant value to the customer. For example, a director may ask for information about a particular market sector. By talking about what he or she wants and why, you might discover that a new product is being developed and the markets for it investigated. You may then be able to demonstrate that the cost of obtaining this vital information (especially if you add value by expanding on his ideas, or offer some analysis) is marginal to the total development cost of the new product.

The pricing part of your plan will also cover the principles by which you price your different services, so that you meet your financial objectives. The main categories are:

- cost recovery, by which you cover your budgeted costs

- loss leaders, if you want to entice a customer in on the "sprat to catch a ackerel" principle. This approach should be used carefully and sparingly (it can restrict later price rises) and only as part of the overall pricing plan, not only for the portfolio of services but also in terms of time. Phasing in a charge for a service can be viewed as a loss leader

- commercial pricing, where you make a profit. The profit-level may be different for different services, but in total you are making the profit required by your objectives

- premium pricing, if you have a service which is in demand, or of such high quality that you are justified in asking customers to pay more.

Place This means the way in which you supply your service to your customers. Do your opening hours suit your customers' needs? Is the help-desk/help-line staffed adequately? When are your specialists available? How long does it take to get the book/journal/article/information? Are the shelves at a reasonable height for most people? What about "browsability" - you may have shelved the stock according to strict Dewey order, but does that make it easy for the customers to find their way around?

People Whether your customers contact you personally, by telephone or electronically, they will be dealing with a person - one of your staff. If you are to establish and maintain the positioning you have determined in your strategy, attract and retain the customers you want and achieve high customer satisfaction ratings, the LIS staff will be the ones to do it. And that takes planning. In the light of your analysis of customer needs, expectations and perceptions, and what the competition is doing, this section of the plan should look at the all-round skill requirement of the LIS - not just their professionalism, but their ability and attitudes to interact with your target customers in the way the strategy demands. Is any additional training required, generally or for individuals? Are there square pegs in round holes? What do you need to do to help them understand what a customer-facing LIS means for them? What performance measures are appropriate, when will they be introduced and how? Becoming marketing-oriented and customer-facing is not just a question of sending out a memo saying that it will happen on such-and-such a date. It is a culture change which needs training and constant reinforcement, by example and action, from the management - you.

Promotion often forms a major part of the action plan. It is essentially the library reaching out to its customers; the humanisation of the marketing plan. This visibility does carry some risks - it can, for example, be expensive, get out of control and not reach the right customer(s). It encompasses all the ways in which you communicate with your market-place, and in any one year the promotional plan will contain a mix of different elements, depending on what you are wanting to achieve. For each element, you should be clear about:

- the target audience
- the reason for it
- the message you want to put over.

All the elements should give a consistent overall picture of the LIS, its positioning and what it offers. Mixed messages confuse customers, and confused customers tend not to be loyal.

The promotional plan will include a mix of long-term items, such as a brochure, and ephemerals such as leaflets or posters about specific events. You should aim for all of them to be in a consistent house-style, so that anyone can immediately recognise where they have come from.

Advice about various forms of promotional activity is given later.

Summary

Any individual action plan - which usually lasts a year or less - will only deal with some of the issues, but they should all relate to the strategy, which may cover a three year period. So, for example, you may set a strategic objective of increasing the capability of the LIS to handle queries in a particular specialist area. One of the actions identified might be to increase the number of specialist subject journals or databases you use. To do so, you have to:

- create the additional space
- re-organise the shelving and equipment
- budget for the additional subscriptions.

This might take 18 months to achieve (i.e. in action plan Year 2), because of the physical work to the library and the knock-on effects on other services.

It should set out in detail the actions which are going to be taken that year to work towards the strategic objectives. All those who are to be involved should be told clearly what they are to do, given deadlines, and progress with the plan should be regularly monitored. And, most important, if some things don't happen as planned - which they won't! - then the plan should be modified, so that progress towards the strategy continues. As with all other types of business planning, the actual plan is not as important as the action taken, as long as the action takes you in the broad direction you want to go.

5. Implementation

You have decided what you are offering and to whom. You know the service is of value - so now is the time to go out and sell it effectively. The marketing planning process has focused your mind on the customer - now it needs to be actioned; the benefits and value communicated.

The implementation of some parts of your marketing plan will be straightforward management-type action. For example, if you have decided that the entrance to the LIS needs improving, you will want to order some new plants, or new notice boards. But the specifically "marketing" elements all have one thing in common - they involve communication, either through talking with people (market research, business development or selling) or through formal promotion.

Market research

The important thing to remember about market research is that it is more than just a random collection of facts and figures. It starts with a clear understanding of what information you need, followed by the collection of raw data, which is in turn interpreted and transformed into a format that matches the original requirement.

Basic information about business customers and competitors - who they are, address, size, names of key individuals is readily available, and should be collected and stored in an easily accessible way. Qualitative information on customers - what they think and want - can best be obtained by asking them. You can employ market researchers to do that for you, at a cost. But the most effective way of collecting the information *you* want, and of raising your library's profile in the process, is to talk to them yourself - on a regular basis if they are existing customers. Make them feel that you care about them and want to understand what they want to achieve so that you can provide an even better service.

Either way, you must be clear before you start about the information you need. Any form of market research interview, by telephone or face-to-face, should be structured, so devise a questionnaire. Writing the questions down enables you to:

- have a checklist of all the information you want
- ask questions in a logical order

- ask "open" questions (how often? which? why?) not "closed" ones (which can be answered by yes or no) e.g. "How often do you use a press cutting service"? not "Do you use a press cutting service"?

You do not have to stick rigidly to your questionnaire, nor should you ask the questions in the formal way you may have written them down - if you are trying to build a relationship with a customer, it is important to let the conversation flow naturally.

Qualitative information about competitors is not so easily obtained. There are a number of good sources; the grapevine, customers ("Who else have you looked to for this service? What did you think of them?"), annual reports, brochures and leaflets about their products and services.

Business development

In the commercial world, business development is a pre-cursor to doing a specific deal. It involves building relationships with key customers, so that they understand what you can do, how it would benefit them to work with you and get to trust you. The idea is that when a specific need arises, yours is the first number they ring to talk about it. It can also be part of product or service development. In such cases, you and the customer work jointly on a project to develop a solution to a need - which they might not have recognised or done anything about if you had not drawn their attention to a skill or service which you have.

This approach is useful to information managers, especially where customers do not fully understand the range of your activities. It is a long-term technique, which may not bring results for months. It is based on a clear understanding of the needs of a small number of key customers, whom you think could bring you a significant amount of business, given the opportunity and encouragement. You then match that with what you can, or could offer, and through dialogue and discussion gradually bring the two together. It can be a very powerful technique, because the customer does not, or should not, feel under strong "selling" pressure.

Selling

Most of the actual selling of your services is done "on the job", by staff responding to enquiries to a standard with which the customer is satisfied (or even "delighted"!). Information people have a head start over many other professions in this aspect of their job - you are trained to do the reference interview. A reference interview

23

includes all the basic elements of good sales technique - questioning and listening to find out the exact need, explaining what can be done in reply and agreeing a course of action.

However, there may also be circumstances in which you want to sell a specific service (perhaps a new database), either generally or to particular individuals. This can be done either through a presentation or in an across-the-table meeting. The rules for either are similar:

- background research. Who are the audience, what are their interests and what action do you want them to take as a result? What are the benefits to them of doing so?

- detailed knowledge of what you are selling, to enable you to answer questions

- careful preparation of what are you going to say, how are you going to say it, and any necessary visual aids. What are the key points you want them to remember?

If you are actually selling something, for example trying to persuade someone to become a subscriber to a premium service, you will often also need to "close the deal", or get them to sign up. This involves spotting when they have heard enough and are ready to make the decision.

Written promotion

There are a number of ground rules in preparing written material, covering, for example, style, paper quality and printing requirements.

Drafting

- keep the language simple; use "get" not "obtain", "help" not "facilitate"

- limit the use of jargon

- be specific; don't pad

- writing, editing and proof reading are distinct activities, ideally undertaken by different people. If you have to do all three, then carry out each one quite separately

- be aware of the different writing styles needed for the various methods of disseminating information, i.e. press releases, newsletters, articles etc.

Appearance

- be consistent - follow the house-style guidelines
- choose the right paper quality, colour and size for the purpose
- decide on the right typeface
- if using commercial printers, discuss specifications with them. They will be also often give useful practical advice, particularly about paper
- if commissioning design, write a clear, comprehensive brief.

Writers' checklist

- is the key selling point in the first line of the text, to encourage people to read on?
- is the headline repeated in the first line? Yes? Then take it out because repetition is just so dull
- will the main message be taken on board in about 15 seconds? No? Rewrite needed; peoples' concentration spans are short
- are there any jargon words or complicated descriptions? Yes? KISS them goodbye. Keep It Simple, Stupid - always use clear, simple language
- are questions posed in such a way to ensure positive answers?
- have you read the copy aloud to check for reader-friendliness?
- are lines of text a maximum of 60 characters long?
- does "you" appear far more frequently than "we"? It should.

More detailed advice about different types of written material is in Appendix 1.

Electronic promotion

Any marketing plan these days needs to consider the use of electronic media. However, the decision to use these media is no different from traditional ones - if your target customers use them and you can put your message across effectively within available resources, include them in your promotional mix. But do not be seduced by hype, especially surrounding the Internet.

Intranets, in particular, can be a valuable tool both for promotion and service delivery. Newsletters, announcements of events or acquisitions as well as Current Awareness Bulletins can all be put on your organisation's Intranet, and full use of electronic media can reinforce your positioning as people who use and understand state-of-the-art electronic sources. The same general rules apply to the drafting of electronic documents as to those going out on paper. The main difference is the increased graphics capability. Coloured computer graphics cost nothing but time to prepare, whereas a full-colour paper document can cost a great deal. However, be wary of the over-use of graphics - most people are familiar with the standard clip-art packages and the effect can be lost.

A number of LIS now have their own home-page on the Internet. This can be a very powerful tool in attracting customers - but only those who have access to the Internet, and are able to use it. As with all other promotional tools, your web-site should:

- reflect your corporate identity
- put across consistent messages
- be well-designed by a specialist
- be kept up-to-date
- be interesting and attractive to the target market segments.

You should also publicise its existence, so that people know where to look.

Media relations

If you offer a service that is available outside your organisation then establishing sound relations with the media can provide you with ways of communicating which are more credible and objective than simple advertising. It is important that the media route you choose is one that is used by your customers - it is too easy, for example, to cultivate only the professional information press. You want to raise customer awareness of what you are offering, and therefore must use the media which they read, watch or listen to.

If you decide that media relations are going to be a useful tool, then you need to develop a good relationship with the journalist(s) so that they will use your material in the way you want. Building these relationships is a painstaking task, needing time and effort from you, to convince them that what you have to say is newsworthy. Don't expect a journalist to take even your existence on board after the first contact - maybe after the third or fourth attempt. You have to work at earning their notice as someone who can be relied on for good accurate copy, a newsworthy story or pithy, informed comment. The journalist's criteria for accepting copy is that it will sell more copies of their publication, so make sure that what you offer is of real interest to a larger audience.

Choose topical subjects, say doing business in the EU, and then angle your knowledge and expertise to that topic. The library might have, for example, an extensive collection of Community trade statistics or a network of contacts with other LIS throughout the Community. Your local business community could benefit from the services; therefore a strategically-placed article in the relevant business pages of the local paper could reap dividends. You will also be recognised as the "expert" in the field, and, if you keep at them, journalists will come to you for comment. They, after all, want an easy life, and you could help to provide that.

Get to know the media

- magazines/journals read by your target market sectors. Choose the right approach for each particular journal, be it press release, hard facts, comment, article or personalised letter
- journalists and their particular interests (maybe even their favourite restaurant!)
- style
- press days
- lead times
- local TV and radio stations (and national if appropriate).

Support your chosen input with an information pack about the library, which could contain, for example:

- a brief description of the library
- a short history of the parent organisation
- details of recent significant events
- a list of key staff, with how to contact them (but make sure they are briefed to answer any questions that come).

Summary

If marketing is a new concept to your library don't be put off by "we've tried it before", "we haven't got the staff to do it", "it's too radical"— this will never win a share of the market or the financial cream cake. The answer is in the planning and the fact that *you* (and your team) are leading from the front.

You achieve success by positively differentiating your service and offerings from the competitions' using your skills to satisfy the customers' needs better.

Attracting and retaining satisfied customers takes effort and is a continuous management process, just like any other. Customers are becoming increasingly demanding. As consumers of many other goods and services in their daily lives, they now expect a wide choice, speedy delivery, easy access and a range of competitive prices. Therefore, your marketing needs careful planning, structuring, execution and evaluation with regular review - just like any other management process.

You should:

- assess   look at the opportunities

                    look at the competition

                    make some predictions

- plan   set realistic objectives

                    define tasks

                    allocate responsibilities

- implement   get the plan going

                    get and allocate resources

- evaluate   compare achievements with objectives

                    explain any differences

                    provide feedback

- start over again!

Appendix 1: Methods of promotion

The library brochure

As this is about the service that you offer, and probably the organisation that you work for, the brochure is a prime candidate for the most uninteresting and therefore unread text of the year! Look at it from the customer's point of view.

Don't be tempted to use the opportunity to turn it into a wordy and worthy description of the LIS and its services - make it short, snappy and to the point, describing the benefits to be gained from using the LIS, followed by the features which bring those benefits.

Concentrate on the reasons *why* someone is likely to use your services - this will help you to identify what benefits you are actually offering. After all, this is what customers want to read about; how the LIS is going to help them solve their problems, improve the quality of their lives or enhance their job performance.

Don't assume that your readership is concerned about the same things as your are, in your capacity as a professional librarian. They probably don't care how things actually come about. So, although you might give technical excellence "10 out of 10" in terms of selling potential, your customer may well consider the fact that the library is open after 5.30pm is the real winner. Did you, for example, buy your washing machine because it had 10 pre-programmed electronic cycles or because it fitted into the space available and toned with the kitchen tiles? What made you choose your car - was it the manufacturers' guarantee that the security system is second to none, or because you can actually get it into the garage without scraping the paintwork?

Start off by jotting down *what* you want to say rather than how you're going to say it. Taking this approach enables you to identify both what to say to attract the customer and what actual benefits you are offering them.

Think about a family of brochures. It can be too complicated and confusing for readers if you try and cram everything about the LIS and its offerings into one brochure. Also it allows you to update information with minimum effort and cost. Develop leaflets about specific services which can be fitted into a folder. If your library is large, include a floor plan and guide to where everything is located. If different people write the copy for the separate leaflets, appoint an editor to ensure an overall consistency of style and presentation.

Every other LIS (and competitor) produces a brochure, so yours needs at least to be as good, if not better or maybe different. Think carefully about your target audience, but unless you really need to be conservative in your approach, then go for a totally non-stereotype style, i.e. no open books, screens, quill pens etc. as a background. Use pictures, graphics, diagrams and satisfied customer comments to illustrate the services that are on offer.

Keep a consistent house-style. It helps to raise and retain your profile with your customer (current or potential) if it is obvious where all the brochures are coming from. It also improves the quality of your image. There is no need to be totally rigid, but if the LIS has an eye-catching logo or strapline, a predominant colour for its paperwork or uses a particular type of finish, then, at the very least, include that in your promotional literature.

You can, of course, use designers and printers to produce upmarket, glossy brochures. This may be a prerequisite of your organisation, required to maintain quality and a certain image. But, particularly with the use of Desk Top Publishing (DTP), information managers should be able to produce literature that is attractive and conveys the right message without spending too much money.

If you decide to use outside designers and printers then discuss the project with at least three of them before you proceed. Design is a very personal thing and you have to be sure that the designer you choose understands what you are wanting to achieve. That way you also get competitive quotes.

And don't forget to distribute the brochures, otherwise they will just sit about on your desk. Make sure they are in the general meeting areas, in induction packs, on the Chairman's table, in like-minded organisations, or put through people's doors or left in the Post Office. The choice of outlet depends on your target audience.

Newsletters

Newsletters give specialised information to limited audiences on a regular basis, with short articles written in an informal style. Those that best accomplish their goals have both audience and content well-targeted.

How your newsletter looks and reads affects how well it accomplishes its objectives. Tangible things such as paper and printing obviously have impact but intangibles such as design and writing matter more. Snazzy paper cannot make up for dull writing or careless editing.

Decide what you are going to include in the newsletter. A newsletter has to be read to be useful, so think of the recipient! There should be a mixture of news (new services, additions to stock) and regular features, for example

- editorial, giving informed and interesting views
- details of relevant conferences etc.
- staff changes
- illustrations, pictures, competitions

Compiling a newsletter takes time and effort, so it is vital to decide in advance who your audience is (as in any other marketing activity), before you start planning the first issue.

To check "readability" ask yourself some pertinent questions, e.g.

- do you know the overall purpose of the newsletter?
- does the newsletter contain more "hard" material than gossip?
- does the newsletter inform readers about the LIS it represents?
- is the content planned in advance?
- are long articles balanced with short articles for variety?
- do you write in the active, not passive voice?
- are bullet points, checklists and numbers used wherever possible?
- does the content inspire and/or amuse instead of preach?
- is the front page attractive?
- do you plan white space into the layout?

Ideally, your answers should be "yes". If they are "no" then rethink that aspect of the newsletter.

You cannot take your readers' interest for granted so your job is to ensure that the newsletter is not thought of as junk mail and put in the bin. Writing is hard work, and it is seldom that you achieve a satisfactory result first time. Also, be prepared to take your editor's pen unmercifully to other people's copy to ensure that the house standard is maintained. Write, rewrite and rewrite again! Ideal conditions for writing include at least a couple of hours at a stretch uninterrupted by calls or any of the other distractions the LIS environment holds.

Because each article must be short and to the point, it often helps to start by composing the headline, to focus on what the article is going to say. It also suggests how important this article is in relation to the others. Headlines summarise and advertise stories, and so should:

- relate to the story
- be specific
- be in the present tense

e.g. "Guide to CD/ROM facilities published" or " Marjorie's Sunshine Wedding".

The best newsletter writing is:

- compact - get to the point
- specific - you want, for example, feedback on the new reader/printer. Write "say what you think by contacting Helen Coote by Friday" rather than "will users please take the opportunity to give feedback to the librarian"

and full of

- strong verbs, they sparkle and are personal. Use "tell" instead of "inform", "cut" rather than "reduce"
- action to build interest
- pronouns, rather than repeated use of names, to help move sentences along.

Posters

Posters can often be the first point of contact for a potential customer. They can be used for highlighting a particular service or event or for a sustained campaign of information drip feeding. The idea is to broadcast a clear message to a group of people, simply and cheaply.

The most important factor to remember when designing a poster is the competition. Notice boards are crammed with bits of paper, so your poster has to stand out from the crowd. It really is worth taking some time over the design and content. Posters need to be:

- eye-catching, because people's scanning attention is brief. Use illustrations, graphics etc. to grab people's attention

- more than just a standard A4 photocopied sheet. Use all the IT facilities at your disposal to create a quality poster; buy good quality paper

- carefully positioned. Choose somewhere a bit different to the staff notice board - in the restaurant, the foyer, on the staircase or even the cloakroom (get in plenty of Bluetac if it's tiled!)

- a short print run. Poster messages get stale.

Also remember to take time-specific posters down after the event, or people will soon ignore them, and the impact of future ones will be lost.

The choice of picture can make or break the message you want to convey. Is, for example, an owl more suitable than a PC screen as a symbol for information gathering? Ensure that whatever illustration you decide to use takes up more space than the words; the passers-by need to keep an image fresh in their mind.

Advertising

Advertising is often a knee-jerk reaction. However, as with any other promotional tool, its cost effectiveness should be carefully assessed at the start. The purpose of an advertisement is to persuade people to act, by contacting you to talk about how you can help them. If an advertising campaign is carefully planned, targeted, designed, carried out over the right time span and properly resourced, it can, for example:

- create awareness of the LIS's name, its offerings and expertise

- help to cement the LIS's place in its intended marketplace

- offer a relatively inexpensive way of reaching lots of potential customers

- act as a reminder that the LIS exists.

What advertising cannot do is:

- communicate complex messages
- answer queries
- actually "sell" the services offered.

Paid external advertising will not be an effective tool for all LIS, particularly if they offer their services only to in-house customers. But many organisations have some type of internal newsletter/newsheet, and it is worth investigating the possibilities of having a regular library column. Apart from including one-off details of opening times, new services etc., you can also use the opportunity to highlight how the LIS can be of benefit to the reader.

In any advertisement it is important to select carefully what message you want to convey and to whom, and so target your audience. What do you want to achieve from the advertisement? Is it just a method of providing information? Is it designed to increase the number of enquiries? Provide back-up for a new image? If you are specific about the objectives of the campaign, then both the design and evaluation of the campaign are far easier.

Who do you want to reach? Existing and/or potential customers? Other organisations? The general public? Your top management? The approach, the medium and the message will be different. What did the segmentation exercise tell you about their characteristics and the benefits they are looking for? This is where your analytical work is applied on a practical basis.

How are you going to achieve getting the right message across? By careful copywriting and selection of the media that you use. The simpler the message, the easier it is for the receiver to understand it.

If you decide to go for a paid campaign and place advertisements in the commercial press, the first stage is to contact each journal for details of the cost, the available formats and deadlines. The cost is likely to be a shock! You should then review the value/scale of your proposed campaign, and look at how you are going to monitor your success rate. It is also worth trying to negotiate a special rate if you are going for a structured, ongoing campaign.

If you are planning a campaign of any substance then it is probably wise to have your advertisements designed by a specialist. But for an *ad hoc*, brief and factual campaign, you should be able to compose the advertisements in-house - remembering to follow the house-style.

LIS "open" sessions

If you have the space, one effective way of raising the barrier between customer and service provider is to open the LIS for special events, out-of-hours meetings, a chance to meet the staff over a glass of wine. There are also the more serious aspects of the conducted tours and the training sessions. These are useful for certain categories of customer, but they should be viewed as opportunities to influence, not just a straightforward exercise in guiding. The customer gets to meet the information staff on a one-to-one basis, and the staff are able to concentrate their efforts on introducing and explaining the services that are of particular relevance (and benefit) to the customer.

The sessions can either be general or specifically targeted at certain customer sectors, existing or potential, internal or external, or a mix of both. They can be either formal or informal, depending on those attending, the message you want to get across and the staff resources. The choice depends on assessing your customer and knowing what you want to achieve. If you have a small area in which five is a crowd then don't shower the invitations like confetti but make the meeting exclusive and use the opportunity to home in on the customer's needs and aspirations, so that he or she gets to understand how useful and friendly you are.

If your organisation runs induction courses for new entrants, ensure that the LIS has a slot. Get them early on, a captive audience, and take the opportunity to sell them the benefits - which doesn't necessarily include a long (and probably to them boring) description of the stock. They are only interested in the end result, and since you will usually be speaking to them at the close of a mind-numbing day of new things, you need to be lively and enthusiastic!

Writing a press release

You don't have to be a genius with words to construct a good press release. It helps, but if you follow a few basic guidelines, practise your skills and are aware of what makes a worthwhile story, then the press release can become one of your most effective marketing tools. It has the added bonus of being one of the cheapest forms of marketing - the only expenditure is your time.

Your press release will be one of a multitude landing on an editor's desk, so it has to stand out from the crowd. If you can get the editor's attention in the first few lines, there is far more likelihood that he or she will read on so long as the story you are telling has a strong and relevant theme and will help sell more of the journal.

Ensure that the information you wish to convey is relevant to the audience of the particular newspaper, journal, radio or TV station. Make life as easy as possible for the editor; concise text in a clear font, typed (preferably double-spaced) on a single A4 sheet with wide margins, including:

- the heading "Press Release". Amazing the number of people that assume an editor knows what it is! It isn't absolutely necessary to have specially pre-printed paper but it does give the communication a certain edge

- a headline, which, depending on the target can be either purely factual, or if you have the flair for it, totally zany - but it must be eye-catching

- a crisp first paragraph which contains all the essential facts:- what, where, why, when, who

- well-written text that is interesting, with supporting facts, figures and photograph (if relevant)

- a contact name, title, address and telephone number

- the date

- a very brief pen picture of the LIS.

Do get someone who cares and knows how to read it through for clarity, reader friendliness and typos.

Don't

- write more than 250 words. The first 100 words (i.e. the first paragraph) will have the most impact

- forget to answer the who, what, where, why and when questions

- pad it out

- use outdated information.

and, above all, *don't be boring!*

Broadcasting

This is a good medium to use to get to a large audience at relatively little cost to the LIS. But you must ascertain that your organisation is happy for their employees to broadcast and whether they require people to be trained first. Even if you are going to talk purely about information matters, your organisation may be commercially sensitive, and prefer you to keep your head down so check on this. However, if you have specialist subject knowledge, and are an expert in your field, then use this exercise to get yourself interviewed or quoted.

Local radio is the easiest to approach and, by its very nature, will probably be more interested in following up a story or what you have to say. Competition is fierce between local stations for audience figures, and so, if you have a genuine story, why be confined to the traditional book review programme slot? Research the potential and make contact in the same way as for the press.

If you are contemplating an approach to national TV or radio then my advice is to contact a PR company for some specialist help in seeking the most effective way about achieving your objectives. You will probably also need some help with your presentation skills.

A potpourri of other suggestions for effective promotion

The library interior

- operate an "open door" policy
- use plenty of clear and visible signs to guide customers
- keep shelf guides up-to-date
- wear a name badge
- organise a display at the entrance on a topical subject that will catch the customer's interest and show you are on the ball.

Speaking engagements

- take every opportunity to speak about the profession, your specific job or the LIS services to internal or external audiences at conferences, seminars and/ or workshops
- contact (if relevant to your work) the local Chamber of Commerce, colleges, schools etc. and offer to speak about your LIS and how it can benefit them.

Exhibitions

- assess the relevance to your work and your budget. Will you, for example, meet prospective new customers, or could you do that in another, perhaps more cost effective way?

- offer to share an exhibition stand with other sections of the organisation or with other like-minded, local bodies

- create a portable LIS stand that can be easily taken to small exhibitions

- go, as an individual, to the large exhibitions, renew contacts and make new ones, find out what's new, who's exhibiting, should you be there next year?

Appendix 2:Case Studies

Introduction

I have included these case studies because they illustrate how marketing theory has been turned into effective marketing practice. The 4 librarians who agreed to have the spotlight turned on them have told it how it really has been for them, an approach that I hope you will appreciate.

I had two major reasons for choosing these LIS: they represent a range of sectors in the information world with varying resources and very different customer bases; and, although the information managers involved take a realistic view of what they are seeking to achieve they also have an entrepreneurial spirit that is reflected in their approach to creating a successful information service.

The case studies are:

- the Library and Information Services of Theodore Goddard, one of London's leading law firms, specialising in business and finance
- Info-Link Business Information Centre, a joint initiative of Somerset Business Link and the County Library Service
- the Library and Information Service of Bristol-based Southmead Health Services, the sixth largest NHS Trust in the UK
- DataDirect, the fee-based business information service of Cambridgeshire Libraries, a pioneering leader in its field.

Case Study 1: The Library and Information Services, Theodore Goddard

Theodore Goddard is a full service European law firm, based in the City of London. The 49 partners cover all aspects of commercial law, focussing particularly on banking and finance, media and communications. Their client base ranges from major multinationals and governments to small private companies and individuals, and a significant proportion of them are based outside the UK. The firm has offices in Brussels, Jersey and Paris.

Paul Pedley is the Manager of Theodore Goddard's Library and Information Services. He joined the firm in 1992 as Property Librarian; became Head Librarian in 1993; and then Manager in 1996, following the amalgamation of the library and information services. Prior to joining the firm, Paul worked for Olympia and York; the Property Services Agency as it was then called and the Department of Trade and Industry. He has had no formal legal training but has always had an interest in legal affairs and soon after his appointment at Theodore Goddard attended the British & Irish Association of Law Librarians' (BIALL) Law for Librarians' course.

The LIS has 9 staff, 4 information units and 4 staffed service points around the building, with 29 PCs and 3 file servers. This serves 300 staff divided into 12 business groups, 50% of whom are fee-earning lawyers. The main library is always open, with an enquiry desk staffed from 9.30am to 5.30pm, Monday to Friday.

A majority of the resources and services provided are typical of a large legal library and include, for example, online, CDs and access to the Net; standard legal texts and reference works; government documents and legislation; an enquiry service for legal, company and business information; a number of current awareness services and regular subject-specific newsletters. What is atypical is that the LIS collects and indexes the firm's internal know how.

Paul firmly believes that the LIS is a key part of the firm, but of course the firm has to view the LIS in the same light. He started in the way he meant to continue, spending a month "temping" as PA to a Finance Director. This was a super opportunity to demonstrate what a "mere Librarian" could do, and during that time he started to build a relationship based on trust and understanding and his presence was accepted as logical. In his role at Olympia & York, Paul attended Directors' meetings - again useful for the future. Now, at Theodore Goddard, Paul asks for (and usually gets) business groups' business plans, is invited to attend their strategy meetings and larger group meetings, and works closely with the training officer with new recruits. His staff also go to "Points of Practice" meetings, and he ensures that he gets to as many of the regular Friday evening drinks and social events as he can. This is all part of keeping as high a profile in the firm as possible and keeping up-to-date with developments so that the LIS can fit into Theodore Goddard's overall strategy.

It was important that Paul knew what all the staff needed, so he devised and circulated a questionnaire. This also included a list of the LIS' functions which staff were asked to rank according to their importance. One of the conclusions drawn was that staff wanted information close at hand, hence the spread of information units around head office and a long loan system of 4 months with the option of the business group buying the publication.

Everyone in the firm has access to E-Mail and this is an important facility for the LIS. To facilitate both speed of response and currency of information, the LIS use it to put up information (such as current legal developments) on a daily basis, and most of the requests come to the LIS either via E-Mail or the telephone. As new files are opened, details of these are given in a "Daily List", so everyone knows what is happening throughout the firm - a good way for the LIS to keep in touch. Also, the Marketing Department produces a regular set of "Marketing Notes" covering work that fee-earners are doing plus any press coverage.

Paul sees networking as the most effective way for the LIS to move forward and keep alongside Theodore Goddard's overall development and he has a number of longer-term projects to support this strategy. The major one, that will reach out to all parts of the firm, is the "Know How" pilot networking exercise; there is also the networking of external systems and the facility to have a copy of the library's catalogue on everyone's desk via their PC. Together with the IT Manager and some senior people in the firm Paul is also assessing a variety of relevant information products and the feasibility of networking them, which resulted in the decision to set up a CD-ROM network which initially gives access to 6 titles.

The LIS uses the Unicorn library management system for acquisition, cataloguing and serials control. Profiles of users' subject interests are recorded and they receive monthly reports of new acquisitions matching their interests. A daily bulletin is sent out by E-Mail covering UK government and European Commission press releases, and details of the latest legal developments. Headnotes of cases heard in the main courts the previous day are E-Mailed to lawyers on the following day. A number of regular searches have been set up with headlines of stories on the topic/company being monitored automatically delivered daily into the user's mailbox.

Networking within the information profession also plays an important role in helping Paul to develop the LIS. He has led developments without any formal IT qualifications and finds keeping in touch with colleagues a valuable way of updating his knowledge of new products, systems and ideas. The LIS is, for example, currently undertaking a benchmarking exercise with similar LIS within different sectors, including James Lang Wootten and KPMG. Paul also gives both formal and informal presentations to other information professionals at conferences and on training courses, as well as writing articles and reviews in the professional journals - which in turn raises Theodore Goddard's profile.

Currently Paul is in the fortunate position that the LIS is seen as a management tool and so does not have to "sell" itself to survive. However, as he sees the operation of the LIS as akin to running a small business, he actually wants to be "profitable" and grow the service. As part of his philosophy that information needs to be seen as another commodity to be paid for - it definitely does not come for free - he introduced a charging system in early 1996 covering enquiries and use of online and CD services; there is a flat fee of £10.00 plus £90.00 per hour of LIS staff time. Paul is also keen eventually to introduce a charging system for the networked information products. The feedback so far is positive, which as the fees directly affect the business groups' profitability is an encouraging start.

When Paul was appointed as Head Librarian, he had a number of key priorities: to establish and maintain a high profile within the firm; to be there and available at times to suit the firm; to listen and respond to requests, introduce new services and amend current ones; and, above all, gain the trust and respect of the partners. But this is all backed by a health warning from Paul, "don't take your eye off the ball, and only offer what you are sure you can deliver".

Paul Pedley can be contacted at Theodore Goddard on +44 (0) 171 880 5899 or by E-Mail at paulpedley@theordoregoddard.co.uk

Case Study 2: Info-Link Business Information Centre

The Info-Link Business Information Centre is a unique joint venture between Business Link SOMERSET and the County Library Service, which offers a fee-based, value-added business information service to companies throughout Somerset. Info-Link was set up in November 1995 (after several years of discussion between the Library Service and the Enterprise Agency/Business Link) with a partnership agreement that the Library Service would provide the Business Link with business information through the Rural Business Information Service based at Bridgwater Reference Library and that Business Link would market the service both internally to Business Advisors and externally to clients, while providing some cash to help with the initial running costs.

A new post of Business Information Manager was created, and Helen Clemow duly joined Info-Link in January 1996. Helen had just returned to the UK from New Zealand where she had spent 9 months as Assistant Manager of a health information centre. Prior to that she had been the first full-time assistant to Nick Parsons at DataDirect, having spent the early part of her career in Cambridge Reference Library as Assistant Librarian for Business Information and Current Awareness. As she had specialised in business information during her postgraduate training at Aberystwyth University, Helen brought to Info-Link a lot of practical experience.

Her initial key objectives were to develop and market Info-Link's current awareness bulletins ("Business Update" and "Rural Update"), help train Business Link's information officers, and set up the Business Link satellite information collections. Added to these was an element of basic general enquiry work but this was destined to decrease as the Business Link staff gained experience and built up expertise. Helen needed the time saved here to concentrate on developing more value-added and income-generating activities; Info-Link had just 3 years to establish itself and, in the meantime, Helen had financial targets to meet.

An initial advantage was that her role had greater credibility at the Business Link than at the public library, but Helen realised that her campaign of raising awareness of what Info-Link could do had to be carefully planned. Her resource constraints were quite formidable; essentially a one-woman band, Helen could not afford to raise customers' expectations and then fail to deliver the level of service they wanted because of lack of staff resources. One restriction was that she had to divide her time between Business Link and her office in the reference library, but this also worked to her advantage in that a good relationship was built up with the reference library staff and they were able to cover her absences. This sort of partnership was key to the success of Info-Link in the early days.

Helen recognised that she needed to "sell" Info-Link's services to two sets of customers; internal ones (Business Link advisors and staff) and external ones (companies and organisations throughout Somerset). In order to do the "selling" effectively, Helen could not afford to bring too many new services on-stream immediately; she needed to strike the right balance between providing the service(s) and promoting them. As with most new ventures, Helen also had to juggle with the general administrative work needed to establish Info-Link, which included getting a licence for photocopying documents, creating the right financial systems and collecting those ever-important statistics.

Rather than re-invent the information wheel, Helen focussed on the two current awareness services that were already available - "Business Update" and "Rural Update". The services are complementary, with the latter title specifically addressing rural issues. Initially, Helen turned her attention to "Business Update", a monthly publication started in November 1995, containing headline abstracts from broadsheet newspapers and journals covering a wide range of business-related interests in the UK and Europe. The abstracts contain the latest news, developments, legislative and policy changes on topics relevant to business, including, for example, employment, innovation, export, taxation and marketing. For an annual fee of £250.00, subscribers received "Business Update"and a maximum of 10 full abstracts giving fuller news on critical or time-sensitive issues.

After an overhaul with her "editor's pen", Helen decided to use "Business Update" as a marketing tool. She selected 200 target companies with a trial run of fortnightly (rather than monthly) editions, and included a simple questionnaire with each copy, with the aim of establishing her potential customers' real information needs. The exercise met with only limited success; 5 new companies decided to subscribe. Undaunted, Helen identified a gap in the Business Link information market - and promptly sent copies to all the other Business Links. As a result, one Link decided to buy in the service and another negotiated to use specific articles. Helen sees "Business Update" as a marketing tool and uses it to advertise the quality and scope of Info-Link's services.

"Rural Update" was not as easy a service to sell as its business counterpart. This was partly due to its potential market; farmers are notoriously difficult to "sell" anything to, never mind an information service. She identified agricultural colleges as an easier market to penetrate, and investigated the feasibility of distributing "Rural Update" to banks, Local Authorities and District Councils, all of which have a vested interest in the rural economy.

Alongside the "Updates", Helen has started to create a small family of descriptive brochures that could be used as a "calling" card and promotional tool. She chose a simple, clear, corporate logo printed on good quality but inexpensive coloured paper that supported the position that Info-Link was taking between the Business Link and the County Library. The information given is concise and crisp with plenty of "white space", and the generic leaflet has a snappy strapline, "Information is Power! - boost your business". It also has the added advantage of having a fax-back sheet that people can use for sending enquiries directly back to Helen.

But Helen recognises that literature is not enough. "I needed to get out there and talk to people, both inside the Business Link and outside in the business community", says Helen. So she joined a number of local business organisations, regularly attending meetings and speaking about Info-Link whenever she was given the chance. She sees information audits as a potential source of income but before she can offer them she needs to build up relationships with local business people, so that they know what she can offer.

"I also need to be accepted as part of the Business Link team", she says, " and the only way to do that is to attend as many internal meetings as possible, contributing when the time is right. Helen offers tours around the business library for Business Advisors and also to people on Business Link start-up courses. It is never too early to get your foot in the door of a young company - it just might be the Microsoft of 2001.

Helen is also trying to develop a relationship with the local press, never an easy option given that information stories rarely set the world on fire. But she has had some success, and so is building on her contact to ensure that Info-Link has the coverage it deserves.

Helen still has a lot to do. She knows that proactivity will help to strengthen Info-Link's position but she needs to temper that with ensuring that she can deliver what she has promised.

Helen can be contacted +44 (0) 1278 436500.

Case Study 3: The Library and Information Service of Southmead Health Services

Bristol's Southmead Health Services gained NHS Trust status on 1 April 1992 and is now one of the largest Trusts in the UK, with over 1,000 beds on one site. Southmead specialises in paediatrics and renal medicine, and both the regional cytogenetics and one of two National blood service sites are based there. The site has been in existence since 1902 and actually started its medical history as the location for Bristol's first workhouse and infirmary.

Currently in Bristol there are 3 substantial health care libraries and in the last few years a number of library contracts have been put out to tender. As a result, Bristol is a good example of the competitive development in healthcare library provision, with librarians having to prepare bids to run a service which a colleague from another library is also offering.

Southmead's Library Information Services Manager is Caroline Plaice, who after qualifying at Aberystwyth moved immediately into working in the healthcare sector. She worked for hospitals in Cardiff and Plymouth before moving to Frenchay Hospital in Bristol as Medical Librarian in 1988. Here she was determined to make the library proactive; she set up a service for paramedics, was the first to introduce CD-ROMS, and also to automate the loan system. During 6 years at Frenchay she was involved in a research project looking at the interaction between the Bristol Healthcare libraries, and also became a supervisor for the Library Associations's Associate programme. (The latter was valuable in a number of ways, not least in that it gave her the opportunity to question why she had done things the way she had.) But the event that really made a difference to how Caroline approached developing a library and information service was winning the contract to run the library service of Bristol & District Health Authority (later Avon Health Authority).

Caroline moved to Southmead in late 1994 to head a multi-disciplinary Library Service that is one unit of the Directorate of Medical Education and funded jointly by the Trust and the Post Graduate Medical Dean. There are 8 staff, of whom 3 are full-time and 1 part-time (qualified staff), who provide a service to people spread over 5 sites. As Southmead comes under a rival Trust Caroline couldn't bring the Avon contract with her, but her goal was to win it for Southmead. She knew already the high standard that Avon set and that the Authority was happy with its current service. She decided that taking the traditional marketing approach was not enough; it would have to be supported by a business development approach.

She needed to build a strong business relationship with her key customer (whose organisation was at a crucial stage in its development) so that he understood the increased level of service that he could have by using Southmead's library.

The first step was a marketing audit (including a SWOT and PEST see pages 11 and 15) of the library, which Caroline did jointly with her team. It highlighted two key skills within the service which had the potential to be developed and used to advantage. These were the ability to attract customers from outside the Trust because of existing extensive IT facilities, and a high level of expertise in setting up SDI services for small, specialised institutions. On the down side, the Library had an overload of paper-based filing systems and a low success rate in satisfying requests for grey literature. From the audit the library's strategy and mission statement evolved.

Stage 2 was to segment the customer base and see whether the Library could satisfy the needs of existing and new customers. It was also important to assess what value any new customers would be to the Library - including Avon Health. After due consideration, Caroline decided to go for the contract and undertook some basic market research. "This is where networking came in very handy" says Caroline. "I updated my knowledge of the Authority by talking to colleagues and visiting a number of other libraries". She also looked at the competition and what they offered, the service given by the current library, and then rated Southmead against them. When the time came for Avon Health to select a provider to run the Library Service, Southmead was one of two services asked to make a presentation.

"Market research is a thread which should constantly run through any service - it comes back to the need to investigate in order to anticipate" says Caroline. And certainly there were a number of key insights she gained from her background research which helped her to construct her presentation. A number of issues that needed careful handling included pricing and availability of the service. She opted for a competitive strategy which would cover costs plus a small additional amount for the first year, and made it clear when a librarian would be on-site at the Authority as well as installing an answering machine at Southmead.

Promotion was also an important part of winning the contract. For example, the panel were invited to visit Southmead to see first-hand the quality of the service and be impressed by the range of IT. Profiles of the staff were produced, highlighting their individual skills and including photographs so that the visitors would be able to recognise individuals. Caroline also built the business relationship by regularly contacting her potential client with relevant information and details of new services which would be of benefit to him.

"Having a strategy undoubtedly enabled us to put in a strong bid" says Caroline - and all the preparation paid off. Southmead won the contract, and in doing so enhanced the Library's image within its own organisation. This has led to Caroline investigating how she can start increasing the library's market penetration within Southmead itself; starting, of course, with a strategy before moving on to developing a marketing plan.

Caroline Plaice can be contacted on +44 (0) 117 959 5345

Case Study 4: DataDirect, the fee-based business information service of Cambridgeshire Libraries

In 1992 Cambridgeshire Libraries went through a major re-structuring exercise, and one of the positive results was the establishment of DataDirect. From reasonably humble beginnings in the Central Library, DataDirect is now widely regarded as one of the most successful fee-based business information services in the public library field.

After completing a degree in economics and economic history, DataDirect's Manager, Nick Parsons, started his career as a graduate trainee in a major High Street bank and came to librarianship purely by chance. He was offered a library assistant's job at Reading University and so enjoyed the process that he completed a postgraduate course at the Polytechnic of North London (now the University of North London). His first professional post was in Cambridge Reference Library, after which he moved around the Library Service gaining experience (and promotion) before setting up DataDirect.

Establishing a high quality fee-based business information service in the early '90's was a serious challenge. He is the first to admit that he did not have the full range of business and marketing skills needed for a librarian to go out and set up what was essentially a new business in the competitive, commercial world. He knew the theory of business planning thanks to his time in the bank but the rest was a result of absorbing theory, practice - and learning by mistakes and talking to other people. He did however have the backing of a superb collection of business material and colleagues' expertise and support.

In the first year Nick's marketing plan focussed on establishing the DataDirect brand and recognition of the name, designing and distributing publicity and then promoting the service to the local business community. A major disadvantage for DataDirect (and one that many new businesses have to handle) was not having a track record; also being associated with the public library did not help its image in the business community. If he had his time over again, Nick would segment his potential market. He now believes his approach was too general, trying to offer all things to all customers - which he acknowledges is usually a recipe for disaster. But since his professional survival depended on DataDirect's success, Nick took a pragmatic approach to marketing (after all, marketing is 90% commonsense) and resigned himself to a year of very little free time.

He needed to generate income, initially to cover his costs. So setting his fee rate was critical but he had no blueprint. He solved the problem by finding out the rates that other professionals (e.g. accountants and solicitors) in the area charged, looking at other information brokers' rates and assessing the perceived value of information. To overcome potential resistance to paying for what had previously been "free" information, Nick focused his publicity material on the value-added service that he offered, highlighting the benefits to the customer of using DataDirect. His aim was for customers to see DataDirect's service as part of *their* product or service development, a professional cost like any other needed to run a successful business.

Promotion played a major role in the early stages of DataDirect's establishment. Nick took every opportunity to speak at meetings and make presentations to groups of business people. At the beginning he made appointments to visit every Council department and he was fortunate to have the backing of a number of local business agencies. "Because of this support", says Nick, "in the early days DataDirect's "Open Evenings" offered businesspeople the opportunity to meet a wide range of advisors, not just me!" It also showed that he could organise events in which other, better-known organisations participated thereby increasing DataDirect's market credence.

He also targetted a number of local companies with literature and then followed up by telephone - all with the aim of getting in to make presentations to them. The first appointment was with a major company but it was almost a lost opportunity as he did not focus clearly enough on the benefits to the company of using DataDirect. Fortunately the MD saw the advantages and is now one of Nick's most valued customers.

The local press were also targetted and the ensuing coverage was good. Nick was fortunate to attract some local dignitaries to DataDirect's launch, and so the event was considered "newsworthy". He built on this by initially holding an event every month, and either inviting the press or issuing press releases - therefore keeping DataDirect's profile high in the local community. In addition to press coverage, Nick regularly used mail shots which, his statistical analysis showed, worked well for him. He was also persuaded to enter business competitions, with a great degree of success, and this led to further press coverage and awareness-raising. In 1996 he won the "Public Library Entrepreneur of the Year" award and the previous year DataDirect took second place in the "Cambridgeshire Small Business Awards" (pipped at the post by a vegetarian sausage -maker).

Slowly, DataDirect started to build up a regular customer base. One of Nick's beliefs is that the customer should always be kept informed. He is always very open and clear as to costing and agrees a level of spend above which the customer does not want him to go without further consultation. Currently, DataDirect has a number of "Call-off" contracts (which means that Nick knows he will be paid for an agreed number of days work) and many of Nick's customers either come through referral or are repeat business. "Partnership is a major issue in Cambridgeshire", says Nick "and this route is certainly the way forward for DataDirect." He has established DataDirect as the first source of business information in the County and, as a result, is now able to enter into negotiations with other agencies which need business information expertise.

Nick Parsons can be contacted on: Tel: +44 (0) 1223 712012; Email ddcam@dial.pipex.com.